water or bread

by

Chris Gonzalez

for
Margot Reilly
and
Donnie Pepe.

thank you

Published by
Human Error Publishing
www.humanerrorpublishing.com
paul@humanerrorpublishing.com

Copyright © 2017
by
Human Error Publishing
&
Chris Gonzalez

All Rights Reserved

ISBN: #
978-0997347210

Human Error Publishing asks that no part of this publication be reproduced or transmitted in any form or by any means electronic or mechanical, including photocopy, recording or information storage or retrieval system without permission in writing from Chris Gonzalez and Human Error Publishing. The reasons for this are to help support the artist.

turkey to damascus	6
privilege	7
one foot in front of the other	8
machine	9
post script	10
where ghosts go	11
my previous bench	12
work	13
commitment	14
roof	16
cupid and buddha	17
unseen	18
grace	19
remembering the south end speedster	20

dementia	21
bridge street cemetery	22
terracotta	23
ode	24
milk	25
against aging	26
scotland	27
the perfect home	28
advice	29
self knowledge	30
joy	31
what clutching her does	32
wisdom	33
love	34

turkey to damascus

his torso emerged from the slowly rising mountain of dirt
his arms flew up at me. he called me the angel.
he pulled himself out of the rubble and collapsed
in my arms. he was my god and was just a boy.

turkey to damascus.

there is a road connecting the body and the corpse.
connecting turkey to damascus. safety to illusion.

a boy once knocked at night and asked me for refuge.
I yawned and scratched my balls and shut the door.

there is a heart that is wide like a minefield.
some tiptoe across to arrive at safety.

there is refuge in your heart.
I may come knocking some night. when I do
I may seem like a ghost but no, I'm not an illusion. I'm just a boy.

apology.

there is a bridge between the tip of the branch and the root.
between I'm sorry and I know. between the eye and the screen.

there was a woman came knocking at my window one night.
asked me for pity.
I sighed, stared a while, opened up a new tab,
clicked back and closed the window.

I may come knocking at your window one night,
when I do I may be boring, but know I'm not a a screen
or a video. I'm a woman and your god.

privilege
(for Eli)

you had a habit of always finding a flute to play at the perfect time.
you had a throne and never sat on the ground.
you had a smile and an eye and a window.
a knack for always brandishing scissors.

you had a primal scream and a habit and a hammer.
you had a swift defensive move with your jacknife.
you had a way of being smug while remaining protective.
a habit like a hunter's hunger.

you were the type to point at that rat by that subway track and crack a joke.
you were the type to take your friends down to that subway to see that rat to crack that joke.

you had a habit of finding play in our aging.
a tattoo on your back that made your mother mad.
you had a womb and a mirror and a pool to plunge into.
you had privilege and a path and a descent.

you had a habit of always picking up your phone.
you had a smile and a prison and an altar.

I had the privilege of knowing you.

one foot in front of the other
(for Eli)

anyone who walked with you through this desert knew it was going to be the end of you.
anyone who survives a trek through a desert doesn't feel accomplishment so much as guilt.

everyone that walked with you into this ocean has planted the seeds of your ghosts.

anyone who has grown up with companions knows there's no accompaniment in this ocean.
anyone who has grown apart from anyone knows that barreling waves of ghosts create thirst.

everyone that walked with you into this desert has spent days digging for water.

nobody that danced with you in your mosh pits or saw you singing thought you'd die like this.
nobody thought they would survive teenhood but believed you, if anyone, would get to get old.

everyone who has tried to harvest one of your ghosts knows no ghosts grow in scathing sand.

the heat that burnt a hole through your arm made you proud. bragging when your charred wounds glowed, you grinned, water falling off the needles of the cacti made you spin and glow and sing.

everyone who pitched a heap of dirt onto that coffin, in that hole, well, they threw a whole ocean on a fire.

as you grow you move us toward the thought that we must live like this,
with one foot in front of the other and into the barreling waves.

where there is no more thirst for becoming.
anyone who knows you knows you are going to bring the best of you.

we know that you are growing and we know that you are not.

machine

your naked toe renews a love of warmth
and a refusal to let go of summer

summoning a sickening wind
which jumps from each tree's spine to spin
sucking our youth and green skulls into the earth for a time

it is the lack of effort that forces spirit through the matter
showing each machine to be a mess of thought and lies

post script
(for Abaddon and Aurelia)

Abaddon was the least articulate husband she'd had. "good night, my love," she'd say and he'd get flustered. he'd pace around and start to stutter, finally collapsing beside her on their bed, mumbling in frustration. still, Abaddon was the closest friend she'd made. he brought her to their park bench during her depressive episodes, and where her ex- husbands would have lectured her, or leaned back knowingly, Abaddon slumped forward like she slumped forward, and he never thought to say a damn thing.

Abaddon was the least obsessive painter she'd married. he only finished six works, all of which (even those dedicated to Aurelia) failed. still, Abaddon was the closest thing to a creative genius she'd known, and where her ex- husbands would have condescended to her prosody and poems, Abaddon always laughed at the right parts. Abaddon and Aurelia will be found on any park bench in every park, he will be the one at a loss for words, she will be the one who leans to listen at his heart.

where ghosts go

the first time I died I went, like an idiot, to my gravestone. there was literally no one there for nine days. I didn't get a pamphlet. there were no neatly assembled directions showing me where to go, there certainly were no wise spirit guides. the only soul in sight was a lawn mower man who moved his lips silently while he composed mediocre poetry. after fifteen minutes I supposed I should stop simply being nothing and haunt him or something. I concentrated my mind on slowly opening the door of his pickup truck and then slamming it closed while he started the mower. I did with relative ease. he didn't look up. he calmly said, "d'ya just die?" (myself was a silent affirmation) then he was eerily kind. "yea, you just died. just so you know, this isn't where ghosts go." then I remembered real graveyards are carried step by step, beat by beat by heart where loved ones can hardly be forgotten! so I went downtown to my son's favorite bar.

I saw him sitting at a round table alone in the middle of the room, staring at the juke box. I tried to get his attention, but his eyes were fixed forward as he swigged and sighed. he finally said, as if to the wall, "no one has ever died that was as close to me as my dad. I guess he's with me in spirit, right? in my heart, right?" none of the barflies looked at him but they all said at once, "man, that ain't where ghosts go." then they toasted, swigged and sighed. the bartender didn't look up from switching the kicked keg but said kindly, "kid, whadda these assholes know? so long as your ol' man is remembered, he's alive!" but my son wasn't listening. he just stared at the jukebox, swigged and sighed. truth be told, I wasn't in his heart. I found it hard to love him because, impatiently, and selfishly, I mainly wondered how long he could keep me in mind. how long before I faded beyond the reach of our most sentimental memories, and became that aimless grief that lives beneath his train of thought, like a bum under the tracks?

the most terrifying thing about being a ghost is if you fail to find stable housing within the first four months you are deported back to embodiment. there is a tyrannical, spiritual force that finds you wherever you're hiding, and drags you back over the border of skin, bone, hair, breath. the first time I died I was deported back to this body. I arrived with nothing, not even a name. since then, I have built myself houses of sounds and stories. so next time I die, perhaps I'll have someplace to stay.

my previous bench

I bet his pessimistic temperament propelled him here. that man sitting on the bench with his briefcase and pen. scratching in his notepad. probably his bad attitude made his family ask him to move so now he is just brooding on a bench at the amtrak. trying to choose where to begin again, fumbling with maps and magnifying glasses, tracing lines on stained papers spread over his lap like he is going to begin again. I bet his name is boring like Bill, or more likely, Allen. something so plain it made his family ask him to move. but then again what've I got to prove and to whom? why do I need a Bill or an Allen? I stroll over to meet him. I'm done judging books by their covers. I extend my hand and I ask him his name, he says, "Bill, but most people call me Allen." I ask, " what brought here for this train? where you are going and why?" he laughs and says "it's not so interesting. I'm going to north carolina to die." I say, "please Bill or Allen, don't hold back, tell me more." he says, "my wife and my kids had an intervention last week, and decided it'd be best if I left because I'm a slob and a bore." I say, "unfortunately that's true." as I get up and return to my previous bench. I return to judging books by their covers because covers are convenient.

work

work to work
apply to work to make money
work to apply money to life
to keep working for life
to work to make a life
work for money more money
no work. I deserve, I deserve
I deserve hard work
the way it works
is like work sucks but it suffices
to make life work
suffering is life's work
Janis Joplin sang
work me, lord
she sang blues
suffering though
her spirit grew
she changed heart with voice
her work was her life
her health suffered
and some say
suffering brought her closer
to the source
nothing particularly
glamorous about hell
though in hell we change
heart with voice and we work
our way through.

commitment

I'm just a blind emcee
seeking the soothsayer's cypher
freestyling into my walking stick
I am anonymous in these woods
I am my own sangha

wandering from bonfire to bonfire
I seek a guild of griots convening
nightly, I hear there is a band
of blind emcee's who see rightly

I hear they're able to sacrifice
their interpersonal fears to carry a collective
flow, and if you're too frightened
to unfold your untold wisdom
motherfucker you've got to go

so I have been practicing
by freestyling into my walking stick
and when I swing it thru the air
I am inquiring
I rely upon the stillness of dead stumps and stones
to get the clearest picture of the pitch black
it all takes shape when my stick smacks
vibrations creep and concretize
and paths begin to form
fogged and iridescent

(darkness forgives my foolishness
and loves me when I question)

lately I've been freestyling
into my microphone
and when I sing into the air
I am desiring
I rely upon transient spoken words and hope to peek
the design within the darkness
is a mind I woke to speak to

(so I will keep true to the foolishness in question)

so if I ever do I find the elusive emcee's
and commune with un-accommodated poets
I will show them I woke to speak in rhymes that outline a shapeshifting
abyss

I'll let the metronome of crackling flame forge me a map
I'll let it lead me where meek peace bringers rap

I'll sacrifice fickle fears
to practice all these coming years

I will see my own foolishness through from shade to shape

roof

the kid spray paints "dharma love" in dull graffiti at the neurotic moon. sipping forty's on top of the opera house. violins cannot be plucked over her thought process unless their strings be taught. else vibrations be lost in the room, often be ghosts of dead composers that float up through the roof, like Beethoven in his black hoodie and black boots. or Chopin, bobbing his head, obeying a metronome which had long since been said to say nothing about time. they watch they kid shake up her spray paint and mutter her rhymes. they watch her as she holds up her can, rejecting its contents at the motionless composition trapped in the image of the city, and manifests the rhythm in her wrists, and permits her abstracted thoughts to exist unobstructed.

I heard she creeps to the roof in secret. that the music below her feet never penetrates her soul. it does not subdue the doves that hum in halo above her dome, so in madness she wields dual spray cans and splatters "dharma love" at the opaque astrology of night, then calls it a day. the specters gather behind her, eyes all transfixed on her mural, as it hangs, like amoebic melatonin above drowsy bare trees. the jade and the yellow twist together and swell a swollen purple. she blushes as the withdrawn shades of moon down play off of grey fog and get tangled up in blue. this is the perfection of the city's deathless genius. the violins seem a slew of un-salivated tongues, thus, thugged out spirits come, from beyond the grave to watch the kid do what must be done for dharma's sake. in desperation, the moon accepts her prayer. she washes down the lukewarm dregs. she is absolved above the city. she makes her peace, tonight.

cupid and buddha

at the center of a labyrinth hedge maze, laid cupid, with his headphones plugged in the belly button of the buddha, who sat crossed legged in an ashtray expounding sutras, slurring sanskrit, lips dribbling juice of the pure lotus root. cupid's mind was tortured. he held up an orchid and said, "this, benevolent buddha, I shall never be: irrelevant. for I am love or at best a symbol of love so my metaphor is evident only to those who sleep on shafts of sun beams, and even the lonely only know me as fleeting. I am the furnace in which their fire is feeding, their dire needs and desires breeding, but me, I'm just a baby. buddha say me some scripture, say me some rhyme, that will rip open my cocoon to butterfly bloom the true essence of timeless, moon dusted love."

buddha's eyes sank low like a moon dusted thug. he said, "what you must understand is that transience will thieve all notions of you. mankind will drown in translucent oceans of truth, save the ones that understand that there is beauty in blue. if you sail the sea and fail to see the beauty is you, you might wind up looking for it elsewhere, crawling around some hedge maze, like a baby." at that cupid paused. he reached into his diapers, he pulled out a pistol. he said, "this is all I've ever found in this place. sometimes I put it in my mouth and imagine the sound that it makes like a loud detachment, like I can hear one big bang that collapses the walls of the labyrinth. buddha, the nature of quiet escapes me, desire and hatred create me in their likeness. I'm like a baby. phantom pains float out my brain and are the strangers I don't believe in, and when I close my eyes I see them, bent and bewildered like wilting flowers afraid to transcend reason."

buddha said, "behold your mind is in season to bud the drugs in needs to acknowledge itself. your freedom in knowledge itself. so hold this moment, this flower like it is everything you've always been without. like it is all that you have, you have everything, now." cupid cocked back the gun that he held in his mouth and he wasted himself mid nirvana. buddha's blood spattered face remained still, he picked up the orchid, beginning to wilt. struggling to remember his in breath, he said, "may babies be born tonight."

unseen

the number appearing on your phone is the poem
                                                the person calling you is yourself
all you need is the number and you can trace the call
                                                hopefully.
if a stranger keeps calling you
                      only to sigh and hang up
                                        that's me.

grace

grace because this wind is unforgiving
the burning of your guilt is not enough
hope because birds spring up from dust
grace because love is just beginning.

I hear you step on snapping branches
I see you hunched to grab clumps of twigs at your toes
I know you watch the wind carry a bird above your head
before it dives into the pyre in your soul.

hate when the birds carry strings in their mouths
to burn or to forgive is not enough
rage and the trees release the birds they've clutched
happiness when the birds unravel us then send us spinning.

I hear you throwing something on your pyre
singing, teary eyed, picking up your mess
I know you've watched the wind carry the bird
pulling the flames with the apologies that burst from your chest.

hope because the agony is air born
grace because this breeze douses that flame
hate because this mess is your fault
rage and I fly from your chest like smoke.

remembering the south end speedster

donnie pepe used to be known as the south end speedster
because he was always running at the rapidly receding finish line
that divided the darkness of his past from his foreseeable future

although recently he will be found crawling
through the cool ashes and embers of what's never happened
his eyes are still sprinting. I call donnie pepe my father
because he asked me to carry his light round the bend

I push my father out onto a balcony that overlooks his city
through his rusty iron cage he counts how many birds
are in ascension, and laughs as they carry brief light up to him

donnie pepe is now known as pepe or pepo
he has stopped running at the rapidly receding finish line
that divides him from the darkness and he no longer chases a foreseeable future

I push my father's wheelchair toward the end of his hallway
we make sure to look in each room or into each person's eye
my father carries himself lightly like parking lot birds

no pepo doesn't run anymore
but he smiles like he knows what must die

dementia

constellations every night feel fake and insecure
because they're cut with shaky knives of names to make meaning
once they're given shape they are ashamed and unsure
when they're observed by name serving beings.

I wish you were your city night again and didn't know

that a synapse drips its embers and embarrassed, sputters out
recognition is a blazing neuron branch that frees my name
now you're cold as an old damp stump and I'm stupid
I remember you-no- I remember that, sure.

now a flood tide's flung from your tongue twisted moon
and my dancing name is doused to the ember of your glance
your deeper roots reach for the knowledge of your sun
but my name won't come, the flames recede into the branch.

I wish you were your city night again and couldn't see
celestial shapes above you nameless ignorant of what you want
I wish the stars fell from me and that you didn't have to know.

what could you do, after you, but forget and glow?

bridge street cemetery

holding onto circles of gardens and fires
thickens the skin we need to grow and burn

we can ride a wheel of fire and flower if we want to

in anycase we sleepwalk, laugh and blush. gardens and fires
help us let go of the fact that most certainly this joke's on us

you walk laps with me around bridge street cemetery
candles and bouquets at 30 graves. gardens and fires

in anycase we laugh, even at grey indifferent gravel
or at the rusty water rushing through the roots of trees

we hold onto our these circles of gardens and fires
we laugh but we never get the joke

we're just holding onto our cycle of denial and laughter
distance and appeasement

we are free to speak our minds if we want to

in anycase we continue on in silence like ghosts

terracotta

loss through rows of memory
remember when remember when
loss through diverging lanes
remember when remember when

loss in the lie of growth
gimme that gimme that
effort in the time it takes

a tomb filled with rows of clay molds of real souls
a mind filled with statuesque friendships
remember when remember when
loss through diverging rows

joy in the effort in the time it takes to know
the mind and the tomb of friends
our effort is our freedom by an easy reciprocity

I died for you, you died for me, that's all

ode

in a cramped cattle car just sped from Thereseinstadt,
bound for treblinka, two youths took the time
to trek across the cabin, on the frigid breathless bridge,
and breathe. through the fogged pane of an imagined
window, they viewed the graved river bed beneath,
unpuzzling its tomb to pieces. each youth felt fault lines
give, when frozen continents cracked and slid
to the numbed currents, where the weak masses melted and meant nothing.

in a cramped cattle car, just sped from Warsaw
bound for Dachau, an elder took the time to
draw on Sarah's breast the star of David.
where the dust was stolen doom was spelled.
through the long pain of an imagined kinship
he viewed valor and resistance. he insisted
stars stole death, until his countenance cracked and slid
under a dumb torrent of prayer, where his star sunk and signified nothing.

in a cramped project tenement, just around the corner
two teens took the time to spray paint
their prison walls with scripted portals.
through the mute force of an imagined fame
they faced the wall till they forgot the prison.
as they slid under the white sheets of saints and saviors
who prayed, and loved god, but gave nothing.

make peace and perish where they hide you
and scribe the unclear names that you were given.
make peace and perish, they despise you
the wall dissolved where all our names were written.

this is an ode to my brothers and sisters, there are empty cattle cars coming.
this is an ode for my mystified niggas, there are empty cattle cars coming.

milk

wandering from the back of the black man's jazz club, where the sweaty sax was in sync with the snare drum, where the trumpets were gradually unpacked by the finger plucked bass slapping scat, it made me sick. when I saw them spun drunk dancing their devilish whim, it made me sick, when I saw how a snare drum brought one down like a dog below a girl as she jumped over his back and then they all laughed. I hate that sensual nonsensical degenerate jazz, so I wandered from the back of the black man's jazz club with my despising pistol purposed in my pocket. then I saw him, green eyes cut into silent obsidian his face black as my lustful oblivion. I wanted to grab this flower to smell, to hold, and even to kiss as the symbols washed and rode and crashed our souls to recognition and it made me sick, it made me sick when I saw the hatred I'd preserved in my self same secret I when, oh my feet moved against my will, as I wandered from back of the then I grabbed him, and I went to hit him, but his face was so meek I made motions to kiss him. I went there to kill him but when his slender mouth moved to smile back at me when I laughed I left the pistol for a moment in the back of my mind. I made my way out into winter, as I drifted down the street I found myself still dancing and happily humping the lamp posts, pirouetting on fire hydrants like a freak. I ditched my pistol because it was loaded with my blame and my beliefs. I then became an unmasked madman for a night on the town. and by night, oh god by night there were phantoms standing on the snowy corners that sold me potions in tiny viles, yes, it was vile but I laughed then I dosed them. my eyes pale blue, my young hair golden. me strolling down those snow white streets like a god, my god, my black heart burst open.

then I wandered in the back of a junk house, where I let the acid rain fall into my bare palms so I could wet the dry lips of my imagined lovers, but they all lay sick, on the floor, unmourned, misbegotten. most were gagging at the remembrance of past lives forgotten, some were clenching their jaws in the awful warm light that pooled beneath the window, some were swatting moths away from glass pipes, all ignored my enlightenment. I just wanted to dance. like at the black man's jazz club, like harlem bee bop, all that meat and no potatoes, but these black bodies were lifeless. no rhythm, no romance, just faded mascara streaks down blank faces, and it made me sick when I couldn't quite tell if I'd found myself or erased it. hand in hand I danced myself out into the alley, where I lay awake weeping in a puddle of milk.

against aging

        a bright gray statue against a black sky
        a poem against aging
        a monument against dissolution
        snow melt now we are deep puddle dodging

        dark purple berries on rhye
        gluttons breath like honey milk moaning
        honey beside the table there please
        pass me my phone

        occupy your future and forget where you are
        translate your losses into clarity
        transform your failures into a future smile backwards on time

        build a statue against a black sky
        build a poem against aging
        a monument against dissolution

scotland

as you are pulled downstream
you are likely to anticipate the fat brutal butt bruising stones
that go unseen beneath the water.

even if there aren't any stones
you are likely to clench and to think and to brace against thought.

as you are walking by yourself down hill
you are likely to desire the solidity in every stone you see
and to melt at the smell of their wet ancestry.

the perfect home

the gods told us they could glaze our eyes over at any time, and that all we had to do was ask. we did. when we wandered hand in hand through those haunted woods we grew so afraid of loss we almost thought we'd seen the world as it is.

and so we asked the gods to grant us pardon from decaying growth, from rotting grace. the gods then disclosed their medicinal mantras that made the haunted woods seem like a safer place.

so the wet laying logs stopped disappearing, and the moss stopped stealing stones, and our bond promised it's permanence. and we grew so afraid to live we thought we'd found the perfect home.

but our eyes were so glazed over, and our hearts were kept so safe, that we stopped wandering, and wept, and stood stagnant as trees until tendril roots crept from the tips of our toes and dove deep into dirt beneath the soles of our feet.

we could hear the gods laughing as slimy bark closed up over our skin. we could hear the gods laughing when leafy branches burst from our eyes. now we remember, and wait, and watch life pass in these wooden disguises.

now we hear lovers say, "I think these woods are haunted". we're mute as trees and can't tell them the scariest fact: that in time they will be where they wanted.

advice

most of the advice we give should go unspoken, or at least, sent in private focused prayer. most of the advice we give we only half remember getting from someone almost fully forgotten. or at least, someone we only remember whenever we get to give their advice again.most of the advice I give I give as if at knifepoint. under the pressure of pretending, like poets, like self-professed "sayers" ,"seers" or "knowers". I find myself guessing to fix, fumbling to reveal, embarrassed to remember that the only thing I know is that I must say something.but my kid says he sees through all that. he's 21 and already knows, as of last week, everything there is know about heartbreak. his first love, of course, told him that they loved someone else. which, as far as I am concerned was totally fine, but, of course, he asked me for advice. I shouted, nervous under the pressure of a sudden expectation, "there's so many fish in the sea." I couldn't remember who said that or knew it to be true but still, I gave it to my son as advice. he immediately shouted back "fuck you". I spoke softer, because I wanted him to see I was being sincere, and said, "come with me." he wept all the way down the dock and when we stepped onto the boat a tear slipped from his eye to the water below and I lingered too long, like a poet, wondering if this was a profound moment, but before I could say a knowing word my son whispered "fuck you".

we set sail every day for three months before our eyes finally flashed when the reel finally spun. I flung the rod back, a slimy four footer smacked on the deck. it's face was lonely, tired and entirely depressed. I could barely even brag I was so out of breath, I said "I told you, there are plenty of fish. so many fish." but before I could relish the pride giving good advice to my son, the fish coughed up blood and said " lies! o misery! I am the last one." I took off my shoe to club it to death, but I stopped when it groaned "kill me now please! there are literally no fish left in the sea. if you throw me back, at least come with me, I'll take your corpse as company!" my son walked over to the fish and calmly threw it back overboard. I said, less confidently, "there are plenty of opportunities to get back what you've lost" he said, "that's not true dad, and that's okay."

most of the advice I give I really only half wish to be true and most often it isn't. and that's probably okay.

self knowledge

        you may stand on the shore, beckoning
        in salty fog until the sea starts spouting
        forth animals. yawning, dripping wet.

the tiger by the bear by the hopping bird by the elephant.

        and yet you can't know yourself.

            so you abide

        and let there be a rising tide
        of tigers from the sea.

joy

we are
weak in the violence
kind to core virtues
sleeping fat cattle

keep swaying like bridges

we are
weak in the orange
light cast from the exit sign
slouching young herds

keep swaying like drunks

we are
weak by the apple
bitten core of the body

our muscles now sluggish
unfold slow to wheezing dirt

even now when
we are weak
in joy

what clutching her does

as sea rocks scraped at the bottom of the ship sirens whispered to each other hidden in the haze below the face of the cliff. the captain awoke suddenly, grey wax had run from candle over compass. his first mates fist banged furious, frightened, "captain! o my captain! voices sound in the mist! they ask for your lovely maiden who lay asleep in the brig! I say come ye upon deck whilst me and the rest make sure she's well hid!" the captain sprung upon his desk and said, "this vessel shall live. and that maiden is mine, so, she shall answer for this." "but captain! you're the captain! no disrespect but you must protect that which is thy treasure." his baritone exhausted a seal salt sight as the captain replied, " yea. I guess.I say get ye to the girl. I will see to the haunts and hisses which unfurl from the fog. for I am a man. I will stand before god. I will answer the riddle of each unseen fate. for I am man, and so first, I must shave." "but captain! you're the captain! shall we go tell your maiden you're simply afraid? because any time anything spooky ever happens all of sudden it's 'time to shave'."

"shut up fred! do as I say. the sirens that wade in these hallow's call often my name. that which brought us here's the profanities of my own enamoured life." the captain grabbed his long blade, his over coat, his prayer beads, packed some herb in his pipe and said sad to himself, "are we not men?" he said sad to himself, " and even when we were, it wasn't enough, even then." he took a long puffed and pushed open his oaken double doors. winged beasts soared above in a melting magenta. their bent iron beaks utter obscene warnings. he heard faint laughter yet saw not but the orange and purple brine of the sea wash calmly over the rocks. a choir of ghastly voices sang yet he knew not whereof "what has become of your love? what has become of your love?" he drew his long blade, he called for his first mate, but all he heard were moans of disgust. his crew dragged his maidens corpse up and laid it on the floor. her lips had been torn off and her eyelids lost in two deep divots of blood. "what has become of my love? what has become of my love?" the choir sang, "captain, can't you see what clutching her does?" "come out ye bastard devils, show yourself from the depths!" at the moment the fog dissipated, a colossal goddess emerged, her rainbow flesh frosted crystalline sin, her eye sockets were two rotting holes with two moths perched on either rim, their broad backs unfolded lo the captain saw what was within as he said sad to himself, "by god, we are not men."

the goddess before him exhaled hail stones that brought down the main mast and sail so thrashed the ship against coral crags till it was sunk, and sibilant, a floating mass of splintered jagged bits, with sirens nearby, bathing, half-bored, lazy eyes above gaunt cheekbones gazing as if to say, "you must protect that which is, you must protect that which is" the captain clutched his maiden on a lone plank of wood and said sad to himself, "I am a man, and the vessel shall live."

wisdom

        fistful of change.
        wet signpost.
        rain.

        slush step
        squish step
        slip step
        muck.

        dirty sock smell
        like laundry not done
        for one month.

        little spider web
        and woven cloth
        that's been dyed red
        and silken moss and moth alive in flame.

        unlike rain
        you are wise.
        but you too
        are in the rut.

your veins clogged up with dark lipped yellow leaves.

water walks and stares and breathes.

the hypnotic repetition of the dripping spears of ice
is life's silent solidarity.

water wants to learn how to proceed.

love

give me time
give me time
I gave you mine

Chris Gonzalez can be contacted at waterorbread@gmail.com

www.ingramcontent.com/pod-product-compliance
Lightning Source LLC
Chambersburg PA
CBHW021002090426
42736CB00010B/1424